THE WESTMINSTER TANNER–McMURRIN LECTURES
ON THE HISTORY AND PHILOSOPHY OF RELIGION
AT WESTMINSTER COLLEGE

The Westminster Tanner–McMurrin Lectures
on the
History and Philosophy of Religion
at Westminster College

II
1990

PAUL M. VAN BUREN

Director, Center for Ethics and Religious Pluralism,
Shalom Institute in Jerusalem
Honorarprofessor, University of Heidelberg

Westminster College of Salt Lake City

Distributed by:

OFFICE OF THE PRESIDENT
WESTMINSTER COLLEGE OF SALT LAKE CITY
1840 South 1300 East
Salt Lake City, Utah 84105-3697
(801) 488-4299.

Edited and produced for Westminster College by
MCMURRIN–HENRIKSEN BOOKS.
Typeset in hot metal Intertype Garamond.
Printed by Publishers Press, Salt Lake City, and bound by
Roswell Book Binding, Phoenix, Arizona.

This paper meets the standards for permanence and durability
established by the Committee on Production Guidelines for
Book Longevity of the Council on Library Resources.

ISSN 1049-9792

THE WESTMINSTER TANNER–McMURRIN
LECTURE SERIES

The Westminster Tanner–McMurrin lectures on the History and Philosophy of Religion were established at Westminster College of Salt Lake City in 1987 as a means of bringing major scholars in the history and philosophy of religion to deliver public lectures and conduct seminars on basic problems in religious thought and practice.

The lecturers are appointed for the national and international recognition of their scholarly achievements without regard to ethnic, national, religious, or ideological considerations.

The lectures are open to the public without charge, and the lecturer conducts seminars in which others who have special interests relating to the subject of the lectures participate by invitation. The lectures are published and made available to libraries and the general public.

The lecture series is administered by the President of Westminster College, who chairs a select committee responsible for lectureship policies and the selection of the lecturers. The Lectureship is funded in perpetuity by an endowment gift from Obert Clark Tanner, Professor Emeritus of Philosophy at the University of Utah, and Grace Adams Tanner. The Lectureship is named in honor of Dr. Sterling M. McMurrin, who is E. E. Ericksen Distinguished Professor Emeritus at the University of Utah and a former United States Commissioner of Education. Dr. McMurrin is a Trustee of Westminster College and a colleague of Dr. Tanner.

THE SEMINAR PARTICIPANTS

February 16, 1990

DR. STANFORD CAZIER, MODERATOR

President, Utah State University

THE REVEREND CANON FRAZER CROCKER

The Episcopal Diocese of Utah

DR. STEVE EPPERSON

*Curator, Church Museum of History and Art,
The Church of Jesus Christ of Latter-day Saints*

THE REVEREND DR. MAX E. GLENN

Executive Minister, Shared Ministry in Utah

THE VERY REVEREND JOACHIM HATZIDAKIS

Pastor, Greek Orthodox Community of Utah

THE REVEREND DR. CAROLYN TANNER IRISH

*Who has served as an Episcopal Priest,
Dioceses of Michigan, Virginia, and Washington, D.C.*

DR. COLLEEN McDANNELL

*Sterling M. McMurrin Chair in Religious Study
and Associate Professor of History, University of Utah*

THE REVEREND DR. HORACE McMULLEN

Pastor of Counseling Ministry, Wasatch Presbyterian Church

THE REVEREND DR. M. FRANCIS MANNION

Rector, Cathedral of the Madeleine

DR. JENNINGS G. OLSON

Professor Emeritus of Philosophy, Weber State College

ELDER HUGH W. PINNOCK

Member of the First Quorum of the Seventy,
The Church of Jesus Christ of Latter-day Saints

DR. MICHAEL POPICH

Chair, Philosophy and Religion, Westminster College of Salt Lake City

DR. DENNIS L THOMPSON

Associate Academic Vice President, Brigham Young University

RABBI FREDERICK L. WENGER

Congregation Kol Ami

THE REVEREND DR. PAUL M. VAN BUREN

Director, Center for Ethics and Religious Pluralism, Shalom Institute
in Jerusalem, and Honorarprofessor, University of Heidelberg

THE SELECTION COMMITTEE

CHARLES H. DICK
CHAIR

President, Westminster College of Salt Lake City

CAROLYN TANNER IRISH

Who has served as an Episcopal Priest,
Dioceses of Michigan, Virginia, and Washington, D.C.

WILLIAM SMART

Retired Senior Editor, Deseret News
Salt Lake City, Utah

STEPHEN BAAR

Vice President for Academic Affairs and Dean of the Faculty,
Westminster College of Salt Lake City

MICHAEL POPICH

Chair, Philosophy and Religion,
Westminster College of Salt Lake City

The Change in the Church's Understanding of the Jewish People

PAUL M. VAN BUREN

THE WESTMINSTER TANNER–MCMURRIN LECTURES ON THE
HISTORY AND PHILOSOPHY OF RELIGION

Delivered at
Westminster College of Salt Lake City

February 15, 1990

THE REVEREND DR. PAUL VAN BUREN is a director of the Center for Ethics and Religious Pluralism at the Shalom Institute in Jerusalem. He also serves as Honorarprofessor at the University of Heidelberg. Dr. van Buren taught at Temple University in Philadelphia for twenty-two years following seven years at the Episcopal Seminary of the Southwest and three years in the Episcopal parish ministry. He has been a Visiting Professor at Austin Presbyterian Theological Seminary, Andover Newton Theological Seminary, Harvard Divinity School, Union Theological Seminary in New York, and Oxford University. He is a member and past president of the American Theological Society and has served since 1980 on the World Council of Churches' consultation on the Church and the Jewish People; he received the 1989 Sir Sigmund Steinburg Award of the International Council of Christians and Jews.

Dr. van Buren earned a B.A. from Harvard College, an S.T.B. from the Episcopal Theological School, and a D. Theol. from the University of Basel, Switzerland, where he studied under Professor Karl Barth.

Dr. van Buren is the author of numerous articles and books, including *The Secular Meaning of the Gospel* (1963), *The Edges of Language* (1972), *Discerning the Way* (1980), *A Christian Theology of the People Israel* (1983), and *Christ in Context: A Christology for the Jewish-Christian Reality* (1988). The latter three are volumes in a four-volume series entitled *A Theology of the Jewish-Christian Reality*.

I am honored to have been invited to give the Westminster Tanner–McMurrin Lecture this year, and it is a pleasure to be here. As my contribution to the field of the history and philosophy of religion, I want to explore with you a change presently taking place, and one without precedent in the history of world religions: one of them is presently changing its historic understanding of another, indeed, the other that is its closest relative. The change I shall analyze is in the Church's understanding of and teaching concerning the Jewish people. This is not as recent a change as that ushered in by the women's or feminist movement, nor as global as the one leading the churches to speak more of dialogue than of mission, although it is not unrelated to either one. It is, however, of sufficient importance and contemporaneity to serve as a case study that might contribute to our better understanding of major changes in the Church, past, present, and future.

I shall conduct this exploration with the help of a linguistic model, not of my invention, that I began to find helpful several decades ago and which is now not uncommon in theological reflection.[1] *This will serve to tie together my efforts of the last fifteen years to learn some theological lessons from reflecting on the Jewish tradition*[2] *with my earlier efforts to learn something useful from Wittgenstein for doing theology.*[3] *That is, in this paper I shall be speaking of the Church as primarily a linguistic com-*

---

[1] The model is summed up in "On Doing Theology," in *Talk of God: Royal Institute of Philosophy Lectures, Vol. 2, 1967–68* (London: Macmillan, 1969); further developed in *The Edges of Language* (New York: Macmillan, 1972).

[2] The major result: *A Theology of the Jewish-Christian Reality, Parts 1, 2, and 3* (San Francisco: Harper and Row, 1987–88; first published in 1980, 1983, and 1988).

[3] From *The Secular Meaning of the Gospel* (New York: Macmillan, 1963), to *The Edges of Language.*

munity, a community of interpretation, centered around a story, the telling and retelling of which not only constitute a major share of how it uses its time and effort, but also provide the community and its members a sense of who they are, where they come from, and where they are going. I shall be thinking of the teachings of the community, including its dogmas and doctrines, as linguistic rules or grammar designed to guide its members in the art of conforming their talk and behavior to the community's story. Theology, I shall suggest, consists in the critical evaluation of the rules and in developing constructive proposals for their reformulation with the aim of making them more useful. Within the terms of this model, I hope to persuade you that the change presently taking place in the understanding of the Jewish people, and consequently in the churches' relationship to them, is most helpfully described as a change in how the community tells its identity-giving story.

I

An educated audience will need no more than a brief reminder that an actual change is under way. By not later than the middle of the second century, as the *Epistle of Barnabas* and Justin Martyr's *Dialogue with Trypho* show, a theory of supersession was taking hold according to which the Church saw itself as Israel, as the true heir of the story beginning with Abraham, and as the valid owner of what had been Israel's Scriptures. It is ironic that the sole Christian leader of the time to have read those Scriptures as truly Israel's was Marcion. When we come to the writings of Tertullian, the mold of supersession has been set in its anti-Marcionitic form: the inadequacy of the ancient law, which no Christian doubted, was due not to the shortcoming of the God of the Old Testament, but solely to the corruption of the Jews: anti-Judaism had already become the Church's first line of defense against heresy.[4] At its most

---

[4] See David P. Efroymson, "The Patristic Connection," in Alan Davies, ed., *Antisemitism and the Foundations of Christianity* (New York: Paulist Press, 1979).

benign, the teaching of the Church concerning the Jews was that they were to be protected and preserved as a sign of God's favor even for the least favorable, that God was faithful even unto his utterly faithless Israel. More typically, Jews were seen as Christ-killers, and that was to lead the brave men of the First Crusade to ask: Why cross the seas to find and fight the enemies of God when we have them right here at home? That single application of the teaching of contempt resulted in the deaths of an estimated ten thousand Jews of the Rhine Valley. At the heart of the Church's teaching concerning Jews was the thesis that they no longer had a place as Jews within the history of God's ways with this world which had begun with Abraham. The place that ancient Israel had occupied had been taken over by the Church, and the Jewish people would only come back into the story by turning to Christ — which is to say, by joining the Church — now or in the last great day.

Twenty-five years ago, this teaching was beginning to change. The Third Assembly of the World Council of Churches in 1961 and the Second Vatican Council in 1965 firmly rejected the deicide charge against the Jewish people. Without explicitly affirming the continuing Sinai covenant, the Vatican Council did speak of God's love for the Jews in the present tense and denied that they were either rejected or accursed. The Faith and Order Commission of the World Council at its meeting in 1967 confessed itself divided precisely over the question of God's continuing covenant with the Jews apart from the Church. The delegates noted, in explanation, that their conversation on this subject had only just begun, but they concluded that section of their report with the striking judgment: "we realize that in this question the entire self-understanding of the Church is at stake."

Many more statements have been issued, of which to my mind the most interesting theologically are those of the Dutch Reformed Church in 1970, the U.S. National Conference of Catholic Bishops in 1975, the Synod of the Evangelical Church of the Rhineland in 1980, and the Texas Conference of Churches in 1982. And the statements keep on coming, of which those of the Presbyterian and the Episcopal churches are among the most recent.[5] If one follows the tendency of these documents, one might reasonably conclude that a consensus is slowly developing not only that the Jewish Covenant is good and valid, but that therefore any attempt to convert Jews to the Christian faith is to be discouraged. A more clearly definable reversal of Christian teaching would be hard to find. Indeed, it constitutes something of a novelty in the history of world religions, that one of them should come to reverse its understanding of another.

II

I have no interest in arguing the merits of this change, since I believe that argument has neither brought it about nor wins it more adherents. I am, however, interested in understanding it, and to that end, I turn to the linguistic model. In its terms, I ask, what is it that has changed? Is it the linguistic community, the story it tells, its rules for conforming language and other behavior to the story, or its critical reflection on those rules? I think we could say that the change can be located in all four, but that does not clarify matters much. Before we can give a more precise answer, we need to be clearer about these terms and so we need to clarify the model.

It makes sense to think of the Church as a linguistic community and more specifically a community of interpretation, because in this way we come upon a central aspect of what the Church does: it devotes a rather large proportion of its energies to the telling, retelling, and celebration of its story. It does this, moreover, with a primary focus on certain texts which it holds in high regard.

---

[5] For statements of the World Council of Churches and member churches, see *The Theology of the Churches and the Jewish People* (Geneva: WCC Publications, 1988).

The Church, in more traditional terms, has a Sacred Scripture that is the source of much of the vocabulary with which it does just about everything that it does, from worshiping God, to defining its membership, to engaging in political action. In other words, as the Church tells and retells its story, it is engaged, in the light (*nota bene*) of all the other elements that make up its present circumstances, in an unending reinterpretation of those Scriptures and of its past interpretations of them.

The interpretation and reinterpretation of its Scriptures and its tradition has not been carried out by the Church as an end in itself. It has been and continues to be done in the service of what we may call the Church's story. Dietrich Ritschl and George Lindbeck both made use of the term five years ago, drawing, respectively, on its employment in current psychotherapy and literary criticism.[6] Both of them, however, acknowledged the influence of Hans Frei, and all of us who use the term will surely admit our debt to Karl Barth. I am using it here as a short way of speaking of what the Church has to say, what it can tell itself (and anyone else who cares to listen) that is its own. It is not other than what the Church takes to be the story of the Bible prolonged into the present. Or, it is the way the Church tells the Bible's story as its own.

Telling the Bible's story as one's own begins, of course, already in the Scripture itself. Deuteronomy 6:20–25 and 26:5–10 are examples, familiar passages that begin, "*We* were Pharaoh's slaves in Egypt . . . ," and "A wandering Aramean was *my* father . . . ." The story of the past included the teller, and the teller was there in the story of the past. This can also be seen, to mention other examples, in the opening lines of Hosea 11 and in Psalm 136. The writings of the early Christian communities continued the pattern, as Luke's *Magnificat* illustrates. Each of these examples, and many

---

[6] Dietrich Ritschl, *Zur Logik der Theologie* (Munich: Kaiser, 1984); George Lindbeck, *The Nature of Doctrine* (Philadelphia: Westminster, 1984).

more that could be cited, is a short summary of the story that brings it up to and includes the teller. The one telling this tale is announcing his or her own identity in the telling.

The Church developed its own form of confessing God and defining its identity that continued this pattern: its creeds. Indeed, its most characteristic confession, that of the triune God, can be seen as the peculiarly ecclesial form of a pattern that is also characteristic of Jewish liturgy, continuing the biblical confession that the God of the fathers is also our God. Creeds and catechisms provided, respectively, liturgical and pedagogical means by which each generation of the Church could pass on to the next guidelines for conformation to the Church's story.

Finally, to complete this sketch of my linguistic model, I should identify the function of dogma, doctrine, and teaching, and that of theology, before returning to the character and function of the story that inclines me to locate there the change in the Church's understanding of the Jewish people. Dogmas, doctrine, and teaching are names, in descending order of authoritativeness, or perhaps only of venerability, for the Church's rules for how to talk as a Christian. If one would be a Christian, that is, if one would be conformed in word and deed to the Christian story, then, says the Church, there are things you will say, and there are things you will not say. That is, in effect, how the Church worded the canons of its early councils; and if genuine conformation to the Church's story of Jesus as the incarnate Word of the God of Abraham, Isaac, and Jacob is the Church's goal, then it was appropriate to develop these linguistic rules.

A clear distinction that used to be made, between what were called dogmas and what was called doctrine or teaching, seems to me to be premised on a considerably stronger sense of the authority of the Church's magisterium than is in fact workable even in the Roman Catholic Church today. And in practice over the centuries, I think we can say that the creedal formulation of the Church's confession of the triune God, traditionally classified as a dogma, was never separable from *doctrines* of the Trinity that were in fact rather different in the Augustinian West and the Athanasian and Cappadocian East. For the purposes of this investigation, and when set in linguistic terms, I see shades of greater weight or majesty accorded to, and greater antiquity acknowledged in, what are called dogmas than in what would more naturally be called doctrines, or even, for that matter, teachings of the Church. Functionally, however, they are all rules designed to help the story do the job which the Church has always hoped of it: to mold the language and other behavior of Christians to the Church's story.

That brings us finally to theology, which shares with philosophy the dubious distinction of being a field the definition of which is essentially contested. That is to say, it is permanently characteristic of what we call theology that it is forever debating the nature, scope, and methods of its own activity. Nevertheless, I shall hazard one possible definition of the field: theology is the activity in which certain members of the Church test out the efficacy of its rules, and propose reformulations of those rules, to the end that the story might more effectively work in the Church that conformation which the Church has always hoped it will be the means of accomplishing. With that brief definition, I conclude my summary of the linguistic model I shall be using in order to analyze more carefully the key element in it, the concept of the Church's story. I shall begin first with its scope and then look with more care at its functions.

III

The Church's story is marked by being all-encompassing and historically specific. It is all-encompassing in that it begins typically with Creation and points ahead to the Eschaton. This is especially evident in the classic summaries of the Church's story in the so-called Apostles' Creed and the Creed of Nicaea and Constantinople. The Creeds also illustrate the historical specificity of the story: it centers in the figure Jesus of Nazareth, and that in the context of the history of Israel. The historical specificity comes more to the fore in an early hymn preserved in 1 Timothy 3:16, the all-encompassing theme in that of Colossians 1:15–20. Both are present in the hymn of Philippians 2:6–11, and the Church's later hymns are generally a useful source for seeing how, in different times and places, it has summarized its story.

Of more interest for my subject is the function of the story. What does the Church's story do? George Lindbeck says that the distinctive function of a religious story, in contrast to other interpretive schemes, is that it is told with a view to "identifying and describing what is taken to be 'more important than everything else in the universe' [quoting William Christian] and to organizing all of life, including both behavior and beliefs, in relation to this." [7] In short, the function of the Church's story is to say who its God is and who and what it is trying to be. Dietrich Ritschl said about the same, but he seems to have reversed the order, the story saying first who the speaker is and then who God is.[8] I do not wish to make too much of this possible difference, since neither author has been crystal clear on the matter. What I do want to bring out that seems to me insufficiently developed by either Ritschl or Lindbeck is that the Christian community has intended with its story also to tell itself or others how it thinks things are. To put it frankly, I would say that in telling its story, the Church has believed that it was telling a true story. Now, if we could only figure out the proper analysis of that sentence, we might find out what it means!

Before coming to that, I should first underscore what I believe to be important in the theses of Lindbeck and Ritschl: the Church's

[7] Lindbeck, *The Nature of Doctrine*, p. 32f.

[8] Ritschl, *Zur Logik der Theologie*, pp. 45ff.

story is its way of saying who God is and who it is. I should think it reasonably obvious to anyone pondering those two claims that they are two sides of one coin, a point brought out by Martin Luther in his *Greater Catechism* by saying that to acknowledge that I put my trust in X is equivalent to confessing that X is my God. And Calvin made much the same point by beginning the final edition of his *Institutes* with a discussion of the inseparability of our knowledge of God and of ourselves. A community can hardly identify what matters more than anything else in the world without making it fairly clear where it stands, how it understands itself, and therefore the identity of that community. I think that those analysts of so-called religious language who have thought that confessional (and, be it noted, basically doxological) affirmations of God were to be treated simply as propositions about what is the case out there, if I may put it so, and not also and always as self-identifications, have utterly missed the character of what religion is all about. Ritschl and Lindbeck have not made that mistake.

There is, however, another side to this, one that I first tried to bring out in a paper published twenty years ago.[9] In telling their story, Christians surely think that they are telling a true story, that their story is about the real world, so that in this story they are saying how things really are. The words 'real' and 'really' need to be noticed. They are clues that we are dealing with a claim that is logically of a metaphysical sort. That is to say, to claim that this is how things *really* are, as distinct from saying what there is, is a bid for our agreement to a fundamental way of seeing things, all things, including what is to count as evidence for the confirmation or disaffirmation of this way of seeing. As I once put it, "Metaphysics does not give us something new to see (such as 'being itself' or 'the ground of being') in any other way than by giving

---

[9] "On Doing Theology," in *Talk of God: Royal Institute of Philosophy Lectures, Vol. 2, 1967–68* (London: Macmillan, 1969).

us a new way to see what we have been looking at all along." [10]
Metaphysical proposals, such as "Everything you see is really only
a copy of its true heavenly form"; or, "they are mere facts"; or,
"they are creatures of the one God," are differing invitations to
adopt a way of seeing that each includes its own rules of evidence.
That is why metaphysical differences are so hard to settle. But
even though they are hard to settle and what counts as evidence
is itself part of what would have to be settled, this does not mean
that argument is out of place or that the issue is not a matter of
truth. I judge it to be a misunderstanding of the Church and
Christian faith to say or to imply that the question of truth is out
of order when discussing the Church's story or the rules guiding
speech and conduct toward conformation to that story.

If the issue of truth is in order, however, it is in order with
reference to the story. Christians believe that theirs is a true story
and therefore true in the way in which stories can be true. So it is
worth noting that Christians would affirm that the story of the so-
called prodigal son — in fact the story of a most remarkable father — is a true story in being a true rendering of the character
of the Father of Jesus Christ. By putting it that way I hope I have
made evident that the Church has no way of finding God inde-
pendently of this and the rest of its story, against the definition of
whom it could then test the truth of this particular story. If the
Church's story is true, it is not true in the way an empirical assertion may be true. It is true in the way that stories can be true,
when those stories are told to characterize what is most important
for — and most indicative of the identity of — the one telling the
story. Need we add that one who tells a story in this way will
surely believe that the story is true to reality, not just for the be-
liever, although there is no agreed way in which to settle this?

[10] *Theological Explorations* (New York: Macmillan, 1968), p. 32. My understanding of the logical status of metaphysics statements is derived primarily from the
work of John Wisdom, former professor of metaphysics at Cambridge University.
See his *Philosophy and Psycho-analysis* (Oxford: Blackwell, 1953) and *Paradox and
Discovery* (Oxford: Blackwell, 1965).

And we should probably add that today many more Christians than in earlier generations may be willing to grant that the Church's story may not be all there is to say about reality or about what matters most, and that other stories told in other traditions may add something of which the Church has not been so aware.

To sum up this functional analysis of the concept of story, I would say that, formally speaking, the story which the Church tells functions to characterize God, to define Christian identity, and to tell how things really are. To ask whether the story is true takes us to its substance or content. It is to ask, is God really the Creator of this world? Has God really given his Torah through Moses to Israel? Has God's Word really happened as the Jew of Nazareth? Are we, Jews and Christians, really called to serve this God? We are already at the point at which the change in the Church's understanding of the Jewish people and its relationship to them is coming to the fore. We are at the point where we need to ask how the Church tells its story.

IV

Let us recall certain features of the way the Church used to tell its story, from at least sometime in the second century until at least the middle of the twentieth century. Israel was always part of the story, but Israel was spoken of in the past tense. Now and then, not Israel but "the Jews" would appear in negative asides in the present tense, not so much as having a present identity, but as the heirs of a curse pronounced upon their ancestors. In popular versions of the story, "the Jews" would appear from time to time as demonic figures, or as a disease that might contaminate one. Rarely, "the Jews" might be spoken of in the future tense, in connection with the End, when even "the Jews" would learn the truth to which they had so stubbornly blinded themselves. But the character of the Church's story, insofar as Israel was part of it, is not misleadingly captured by saying that Israel was spoken of in the past tense. Israel — the Jewish people — drops out of the storyline when it and the Church part company in the first century. To rephrase the point made earlier on, in the Church's story the Jewish people was displaced by the Church as the sole legitimate representative — and successor — of Israel.

Now consider what is being said today: the story still runs from Creation to Eschaton, and Jesus is still at the center. The God of Abraham, Isaac, and Jacob remains the chief person in the story, although God is less liable to be named by pronouncing the Hebrew Tetragrammaton and more usually as "the Lord" or "Adonai," or even as "*HaShem*," namely, as God is named by Jews. And that alteration is a sign of the most conspicuous change: the Jews are back in the story and it is now maintained that they have been there all along. Indeed, it is now being said that the covenant between God and the Jewish people is eternal, as binding on both parties *post Christi natum* as ever it was before, and that that covenant is what the Jewish people recognize it to be: the covenant of Sinai. A number of Christians and a few churches are even beginning to say that any attempt to convert Jews to Christianity is a denial of the validity of that covenant and so a sacrilegious act.

What has happened to the Church's story? It is in important respects the same story, for it has the same beginning, dramatis personae, plot, and ending. It has, however, received a notable addition: the story of the Jewish people, from the first century up to the present, has come in. One could almost say that the long Jewish story was brought in backwards, the most recent events of the founding of the State of Israel and the horror of the *Shoah* pulling all the preceding years in their train, back to the destruction of the Temple, with a radical reappraisal of what had once so unhistorically been called "*Spätjudentum*" — the period of the development following Ezra's reform that was in time to lead by way of the Pharisees to the enduring rabbinic Judaism of the Talmud. In any case, it would be accurate to say that what has happened to the Church's story is that it is now beginning to be told so as to call attention to the existence of the concurrent Jewish story (which can really only be told by Jews), with the clear implication that the Church's story cannot be complete or even correct unless the Jewish story is heard along with it.

What shall we say, then? When an addition of this sort is made to the story, is it still the same story? At the very least, we would have to say that it is surely being told in a different way. We find ourselves now having to deal with a question that is, formally speaking, rather like the one that the Jewish people have had to face for centuries in the light of the Church's use of the Jewish Scriptures: was our Old Testament still their Tanach? If someone borrows your family photo album and pastes in a lot of photos of her own family, would you still call it your family album? But in the case of the Church in the midst of the change we are considering, the Church itself has begun to insist on the hearing of the Jewish story alongside of its own; and here and there one hears it being said that unless that Jewish story is heard, the story of the Church is incomplete or worse. As the Faith and Order Commission said — and on this the delegates did agree — in this question the whole self-understanding of the Church is at stake!

The issue, as many see it, is a deeply moral one. Our old story, or our story as we used to tell it, had an undeniable undertone of anti-Judaism about it, and all too often it was far more than an undertone. If the old story did not lead directly to the *Shoah*, it surely provided a suitable climate for the development of modern antisemitism; and when the *Shoah* did come, the traditional way of telling the story offered little resistance to it. In the face of the *Shoah*, the question is hard to evade: is it defensible morally to belong to the community that tells this story in this way? For many the answer has become: No, not unless we can tell the story in such a way as to insist on a hearing for the Jewish story. Not unless our story is such that it will never again allow us to let Jews stand alone and without allies. Between those who see the issue in these terms, and those who do not see that anything has changed or needs to change because of what has happened in this century, the whole self-understanding of the Church is indeed at stake. For what is at stake is nothing less than the Christian story. What *is* the Church's story? Or, if that puts the question too sharply, then how is the Church to tell its story? Much hangs on our answer.

V

What has become increasingly clear to me over the years is that the concept of story is not quite so innocent as I had once (and, if I read them rightly, as also Lindbeck and Ritschl in 1984) assumed. Lindbeck, for example, spoke of Christians being conformed "to the Jesus Christ depicted in the narrative." [11] Shades of what we used fo call 'Biblical Theology'! Depicted by whom? In whose narrative? Does "the Jesus Christ depicted" refer to the anti-Judaic Jesus in increasing conflict with his people, perhaps the one who calls his fellow Jews sons of the devil? Or does it refer to the Jesus in deepest solidarity with his people as a Jew among Jews? The various narratives "depict" now one, now the other, with many shades in between, and much depends on how the narrative is interpreted. When we speak of story (or narrative), we have changed our terms but we have in no way escaped the issue of interpretation. Like the physicists, we too must include the observer in our description of the observed. Asking what the narrative depicts, or what the Church's story is, is like asking what the Bible really says. Having never met a Bible with lips, I find I have to hear from the mouths of particular Jews or particular Christians what they think the Bible says. Narratives and stories do not depict anything. A teller of the story may depict a number of things. And that is precisely where we are in the midst of this change in which the whole self-understanding of the Church is at stake.

[11] Lindbeck, *The Nature of Doctrine*, p. 120.

Suppose I read the familiar hymn of Philippians 2 as present-
ing Christ as one who, though he was in the image and likeness of
God (just like Adam), did not count equality with God a thing to
be grasped (as Adam did), but emptied himself and took (like
Israel) the form of a servant, . . . even to (a very Jewish) death
on a (Gentile) cross. And that therefore God bestowed on him
his very own name (as he had on Israel), so that all around the
world he would be confessed as Lord, always in such a way as to
give all of the glory to God the Father (just as Jesus himself had
done, refusing even to be called good). Can a Church that is trying to repent of its anti-Judaic past read the hymn in this way?

One could pose the issue so: our traditional exegesis mostly
tells us the story that leads up to and ends with the text we have
before us. The issue in the change through which the Church is
passing today, however, concerns the story that comes after the text
was written, the *Wirkungsgeschichte* of the text. The hymn of
Philippians 2, for example, may have been composed to the glory
of God the Father, but its actual historical use may rather have
been to glorify the Son and therewith the community that wor-
shiped that Son, and that at the expense of another community
that would bow the knee only to the one whom Jesus called Father.
The issue is whether that history may be ignored in deciding today
on how to read the text. To whom or what should the exegete be
responsible? For myself, I see no way around the fact that a story
is always someone's story, told for some purpose, which is another
way of saying that no community can have a sacred scripture that
is not selectively read and particularly interpreted. When we use
the concept 'story,' we are always and immediately face to face
with the issue of how the story is being told.

Never has that been truer than now, in the change presently
taking place. The Church's story used to be told with ancient
Israel playing the role of preparer of the way, and then, having
rejected Jesus, no more to be heard of, with an occasional eschato-

logical mention as the exception. Now the story is being told with Israel continuing up into the present as the Church's fellow witness. Where before, the Church was thought to be the sole means of carrying the biblical story up into the present, now the Jewish people too are said to be this. Note well, this is, I believe, not a different story, but it is certainly the story with a major addition. It is surely being told in a different way.

VI

Then what about the rules? Let's begin with the rules of Nicaea and Chalcedon, for starters. It does not take much probing to see that those rules for how Christians were to speak of the unity and continuity of the work of the one God — from creation through the coming of Christ to the final day — and then of the unity in distinction of God and the man Jesus, were drawn up by and for a Church that had not the least interest in affirming the Jewish people in their eternal covenant with God. The Christian identity which those rules were to help form was one that could be defined without any reference to the Jewish people at all. So the Word became flesh, not a Jew of Nazareth, and what might be called the sociological component of the work of God, her eternal commitment to the people Israel, and the sociological aspect of Jesus, that he was a Jew in solidarity with his people, living under an oppressive occupation, were simply passed over in silence. It should be no surprise that such rules would form a Church that could quite naturally pass over in almost total silence a later attempt of an oppressive tyranny to simply remove all Jews from the face of the earth. Given where and what the Church was in the fourth and fifth centuries, Nicaea and Chalcedon represent perhaps the best choices among those seen as possible at the time. For a Church that means to affirm the Jewish people in the Sinai covenant with God, however, they are simply inadequate.

I think it should be clear that if the Church is going to continue telling its story in a new way, by insisting on the relevance of the story of the Jewish people, then it is going to develop some new rules. We have an interesting example of one in the most recent Vatican letter on racism, which can be read as exploring the possibility of a rule that anti-Zionist talk be regarded as a subset of antisemitic talk, against which a ban was pronounced at the Second Vatican Council.[12] More crucially, the 1980 statement of the Rhineland Synod proposed a new christological rule, instantiated, as Lindbeck would put it, by confessing "Jesus Christ the Jew, who as Israel's Messiah is the Savior of the world and binds the peoples of the world to the people of God."[13] I happen to think that it is not the Church's business to tell Israel who its Messiah is, but the part of this rule that makes more sense to me was underscored when the Synod went on to confess "the permanent election of the Jewish people as the people of God," into whose covenant the Church has been taken by Christ, which shows that new rules for speaking of the work of Christ are inseparably connected with new rules for speaking of the Jewish people and of the Church. I only note at this point that while it is up to Jews to tell their own story, the Church, for the sake of its own identity-giving story, would always have to confess the election of the Jewish people, even if all Jews (rather than just the majority of them!) were to deny this.

And as a final example, I shall quote from the Preamble to the 1982 Statement of the Texas Council of Churches, in which they broke new ground by building on and then adding to traditional rules for speaking of the work of the Holy Spirit:

> From the very beginning God's Spirit has moved over the waters of creation, bringing order out of chaos, light out of darkness, life out of death.

[12] *The New York Times*, February 11, 1989.

[13] This statement (with a slightly different translation of the German) and the following are printed in the collection cited in note 5, above.

It was indeed this same Spirit of God which inspired the ecumenical movement among the churches of Jesus Christ. In our time we have seen the effects of this movement . . . .

There is little doubt that the Spirit of God is once again moving over the waters. From every direction there are reports of a new awareness, a new consciousness, a new understanding between Jews and Christians. In this statement we wish to respond to this newest movement of the Spirit of God and even claim it as our own.

In all three examples, and in many more that could be cited, the old rules are left more or less in place, but new ones are added, which reflects well the fact that the Church's growing new way of telling its story consists in adding to it, not as an option, but as by necessity, room for the story of the Jewish people.[14]

VII

A change by way of addition, however, is nonetheless a change. Since an important function of the Church's story is to define and form the identity of the community and its members (although those who have argued this seem to have thought of identity as something static or having only continuity, in spite of the work of analytic philosophers on the subject), a changed story must be expected to work a change in Christian identity and in Christian self-definition. Indeed, such a change might well be regarded as

---

[14] In the light of comments on the original version of this paper, I can only say that I am acutely aware that I am in part violating the new rule that has arisen in recent years out of interfaith dialogue, and whose spirit I otherwise endorse: always allow the other to define him- or herself. I see no way for the Church to abandon the teaching, in spite of the fact that probably the majority of Jews in the world today deny the assertion, that the Jews are the elect people of God. The Church's story depends on the story of the election of Israel as the Hebrew Scriptures present it. Were the Church to give up this claim, it would face a crisis of identity to which the shifts resulting from the change presently taking place would seem as nothing.

the primary goal of those who have been working to win ecclesial agreement to a revision of the Church's story. What they have wanted was precisely a new Christian identity, one that entailed an affirmation of the Jewish people in their covenant with God, and so one that would be sensitive to the situation and to any threat to the security of the Jewish people. Any change less than that, they have argued, would hardly reflect a metanoia befitting a Church responsible for having infected Western culture with its teaching of contempt for the Jewish people.

If the Church does in fact walk through the door cracked open at Vatican II, it will arrive sooner or later at a new self-definition. As it becomes increasingly aware of the Jewish people as Israel, it will stop calling itself by that name. Least of all will it want to think of itself as the new Israel. Rather, it will see itself as it must if it continues to confess Israel's continuing existence and witness: *as (predominantly) Gentiles drawn through Jesus Christ into that love of God by which her covenant with the Jewish people endures.*

I phrased that definition of a new ecclesial self-understanding with some care, in order to avoid using the problematic expressions, 'a new covenant' and 'a second covenant.' I said instead: "drawn into the love by which the covenant endures." To speak on the one hand of a *new* covenant is problematic because our anti-Judaic tradition, with explicit support from the so-called Epistle to the Hebrews, has given a distinctly pejorative meaning to "the old" that is being contrasted to "the new." To speak on the other of a *second* covenant sounds as if we have something like that which the Jews have, which is absurd. To call the Church's relationship to God through Jesus Christ by the term that refers to Jewish life of Torah fidelity is to ignore or deny the fundamental differences between the two traditions. It seems to me more respectful of both the distinctive Jewish and the distinctive Christian realities to say, then, that the Church has been drawn through Jesus Christ into that love of God by which her covenant with the Jewish people endures. One practical liturgical consequence might be to favor, in celebrating the Eucharist, the cup text of Mark, Matthew, and a number of Lukan manuscripts over the wording of 1 Corinthians and other Lukan versions. Be that as it may, the point I am making about the use of the terms 'new' and 'second' covenant has nothing to do with what God may be able to do, and everything to do with what it is helpful to say.

Since another function of the story is to characterize God, a change in the story will surely change our conception of God, a huge subject on which I can here only touch. The key factor will be that by insisting on a hearing for the Jewish story in telling its own, the Church will begin to have to take the Talmud and the Halakhic tradition seriously. This is bound in time to awaken an awareness of God's covenantal commitment. What will work the greatest change, however, will be the Jewish theme of partnership in the covenant, that God leaves to Israel a major part in determining the future of the story. As a result, it is reasonable to suppose that the long-standing rejection of Synergism will be called into question, the faith/works dichotomy will break down, and Arminianism will have to be reconsidered. All this follows from hearing the Jewish story, in which *HaShem* is a God who has committed himself to operating covenantally and so to *not* working by grace alone. Clearly the Church's theology, in the strict sense of the term, is in for some interesting changes.

When one adds to this the impact of the *Shoah* and the witness of Jewish faith in spite of it, and the founding of the Jewish state without waiting for the Messiah, the Church's traditional understandings of God's omnipotence are clearly in for some rephrasing. Fortunately for the peace of the Church, the women's movement is already shaking up traditional images of power, and doing so apparently even more effectively than process theology. Indeed, I am inclined to suspect that the women's movement may prove to be the major force in carrying through the change we are considering.

VIII

So what now is a theologian to do about all this? I will answer only for myself. I would undercut the whole linguistic framework I have been using were I to presume to say, not to speak of trying to tell the Church, what either the Bible or the tradition "really says." I have likewise tried to be descriptive in speaking of the change taking place in how the Church tells its story. So I have not argued the case for this change, although I surely could not have hidden the fact that I find it morally compelling. I believe it is still barely possible that the Church could turn back from its present course and return to its old anti-Judaic orthodoxy, but I do not think it likely. Consequently, I see the theologial task as having been rather well defined by the Conference of Catholic Bishops in 1975: to work out the implications of requiring a hearing for the Jewish story as integral to the telling of our own, or, in other words, to serve as best one can a Church that wants to repent of its anti-Judaic past, that is coming to see that the covenant between the only God it knows and the Jewish people is "for keeps," and that is beginning to wake up to the fact that this will have to be an essential feature of how it speaks of God.

Theologians can help the Church through the change to which it seems to be increasingly committed by showing that the traditional rules for telling the story, that is, for interpreting Scripture and the tradition, were not so much wrong as inadequate, since the Christ the conformation to whom they were supposed to assist was lacking his *Yiddishkeit* and so in serious danger of becoming a Gnostic Christ rather than the real one. A Church seeking to affirm the Jewish covenant needs better rules than that, and showing that this is needed and that this is possible will make the transition smoother. And that is what I like to think I have been doing these past fifteen years. It has been and continues to be, in my judgment, as challenging and as exciting a time in which to be a theologian of the Gentile Church as any since the first century.

WESTMINSTER COLLEGE OF SALT LAKE CITY

Westminster College of Salt Lake City has been a vital part of Utah's history and educational heritage since 1875. The College was first known as the Presbyterian Preparatory School; later as the Salt Lake Collegiate Institute and Sheldon Jackson College; and, since 1902, as Westminster College. Continued growth and interest in the school and its goals prompted the College to become a four-year liberal arts institution in 1944.

Ownership of the College by the Presbyterian Church ended in 1974, and under the executive direction of a Board of Trustees Westminster became a fully independent, privately-funded, non-denominational liberal arts institution of higher learning.

Westminster College welcomes students of all religious and cultural backgrounds. Two thousand students representing thirty-seven states and twenty-three foreign countries are now enrolled at the College.

There are three schools within the College: the School of Arts and Sciences, the Bill and Vieve Gore School of Business, and the St. Mark's–Westminster School of Nursing and Health Science.

As an institution rooted in the Judaeo-Christian tradition, Westminster seeks to provide an environment that encourages and facilitates the intellectual, spiritual, cultural, and social growth of its students. To this end, the faculty and administration emphasize excellence in teaching, personalized instruction and advising, and flexible delivery systems to meet the needs of students of diverse ages and backgrounds.

Through a course of study that is both broad and intensive, the College expands each student's horizons beyond his or her chosen field of emphasis. In addition to preparing students for a career or profession, the goals of Westminster are to educate students to communicate intelligently; to develop in students an understanding of their social and natural environments; to encourage in students a critical appreciation of the world's literature, arts and religions; to make students aware of the ideas, attitudes, and events which have shaped the past and will shape the future; to foster in students originality and creativity; and to create in students the capacity for rigorous independent thought.

Westminster College of Salt Lake City is pleased and proud to present to the community the benefits of the Westminster Tanner–McMurrin Lectures on the History and Philosophy of Religion.